AUTOLOGY
FINDING THE TRUTH IN YOU

A Guided Journal for Self-Inquiry

AUTOLOGY
FINDING THE TRUTH IN YOU

A Guided Journal for Self-Inquiry

R. A. Shannon

2019

ISBN: 978-0-578-61189-1

S

SAKASH
PUBLISHING

Book Design: Carolyn Vaughan (cvaughandesigns.com)
Cover Design: hmd_gfx

Printed in the USA.

Dedications

This book is dedicated to my son, Khalil, my daughter, Autumn and my brother Warren.

Acknowledgements

Thank you Divine for teaching me that your way is *always* better than mine.

Thank you and a deep, deep bow to the great teachers in my life Joseph Parnell, Emma Parnell, Warren Shannon, Thelma Shannon, Barbara Shannon-Harrison, Floyd Harrison, Bettyanne Shannon, my Spiritual Director Betty Cloughley, and my Baba, Marvin Ponder.

Thank you to my friends and colleagues who have encouraged me every step of the way.

And last but not least, thank you to the readers of this book. It is such a heartfelt pleasure to write for you.

Contents

Whoever knows himself, knows God.

— Elijah Muhammad

A Prayer For You

Divine and holy One, I ask that the seeker reading these words be honored by your Holy Presence and your Holy Word. I ask that as they seek for the truth that is the precious jewel hidden within them, that they and their loved ones are protected by angels on every side. As they turn inward I ask that Holy Spirit be their guide and comforter. Mother and Father God, I ask for their highest good, deepest joy, and that Your peace be with them. Bless them that they may hear and recognize the subtle whisperings and movement of their soul, Your beloved. I testify and bear witness that the more they come to know who they are, the more they truly know You. May Your grace and their gratitude overwhelm their inner dwelling and pour forth into their creations and bless the All that is. On this journey it is Your will and Your way that we seek, surrendering our own will and abandoning our own misunderstanding; the very causes of suffering. Divine and holy Truth, may this seeker be like the evergreen, full of life, outstretched and abundant; neither calling the birds near nor holding them as they leave. May each one be free.

Amen. Amen. Amen.

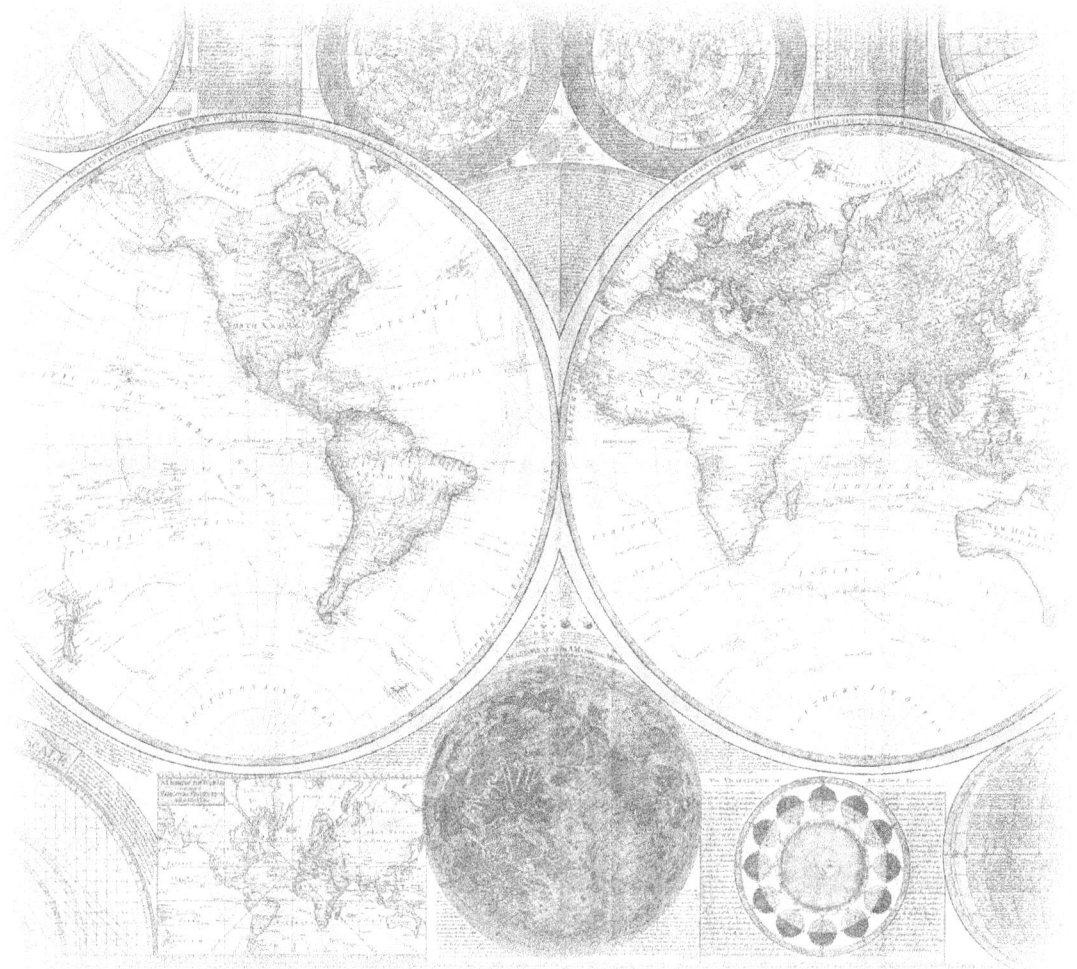

Map for the Journey: How to Use This Guide

In order for Autology to be an effective tool for you, there are a few things that you must consider before you begin.

#1 Autology is the study of one's self, typically used as a tool to self-mastery and the unfoldment of philosophical and/or metaphysical refinement and maturation. It is not a light-hearted, pop culture type inquiry that will tell you which superhero or Disney princess you are most like, or if you belong in the Gryffindor or Ravenclaw house at Hogwarts. Autology requires a strong desire to know oneself beyond mental concepts and ideas. This is a process that is not typically fun for the rational mind. The considerations in this book are not designed for your intellect. Although the mind may try to co-opt your responses so that it can add something to the concepts you have of yourself, Autology is not about adding. The process of self-inquiry is more like subtracting what is not really you from what is authentically you. Sorting the wheat from the chaff, if you will. Our human mind's conditioned response is usually to find methods to manipulate and control whatever current or potential set of circumstances with which it is presented by way of reason, quantification and/or devising techniques in order to obtain safety, security and the best imagined outcome possible; sometimes, for its host's best interest, but always for its own survival. Autology is not the intellect's territory - it is the soul's territory. Autology examines gnosis, our own direct experiential way of knowing. The purpose of the considerations in Autology is to guide you to that deeper space.

#2 The second thing you must be aware of is your natural orientation as a part of life on this planet. There is no one more whole than you. There are only those with greater or less awareness of their wholeness. You are on equal footing with the whole of humanity. It does not matter your age, gender, race, financial status, professional standing, political leanings, religion or how talented you are at one thing or another. There is no one more important than you, and also, there is no one less important than you. The understanding of this is critical to true self-knowing.

#3 You are a creator. You are a creator who creates in every moment. You can't help it. You create even when you're unaware that you are creating. When you enter a room, you create a certain dynamic that changes the atmosphere into something different than it was before you walked in. You create situations for yourself and others - sometimes for the better, sometimes for the worst. You create meals, relationships, opportunities, dilemmas and feelings. In the Bible, it says that we are made in the image and likeness of the Divine, and we are. We are creators. Autology is a means by which you become aware of how and what you create and also whether your creations are life-giving (perpetuating healing and alignment) or life-denying (perpetuating suffering and adversity).

#4 There is a Toolbox at the end of each section. The Toolbox includes helpful directives and practices that you may use to support and fortify your quest for deeper self-knowledge. Every creator uses tools and methods when creating; later in the book, we will talk about the tools available to us as creators. The Toolbox contains useful methods for self-inquiry and creating with intention and purpose.

Lastly, when you write your entries, be very clear and very specific. You are looking for "bottom of the barrel" answers, meaning the answer comes from the deepest part of you and there's nothing left to mull over or consider. When these types of answers come up, you know for sure that what you are saying is true. There is no doubt.

❧

Introduction

This guidebook was created to take you on a journey. I call it the best journey ever because it is about getting to know the deepest part of yourself, your soul. There is no higher purpose than this, because once you discover and align with your truest essence you also find your purpose, truth, power, and a freedom that is nearly impossible to obtain by any other means.

Getting to know your soul is fundamentally different than what we're used to expressing as "knowing ourselves". Normally, when we think of who we are, we may think something like: My name is Sam and I'm married with 3 kids. I'm educated because I have a degree from Such & Such University. I've done quite well for my family and myself, as I am an Architect with Such & Such firm and I live in a good-sized 4 bedroom home in Such & Such neighborhood. This way of knowing ourselves is only describing the veneer of one's existence. Beneath this smooth and shiny surface are several layers that must be infiltrated and exposed in order to gain access to the soul, the true self. This journey is hard work, and truly knowing yourself goes a lot deeper than knowing that you prefer bleu cheese to ranch dressing on your hot wings.

What Exactly is Autology?

The root word, auto-, has its origin in the Greek language and simply means "self." The suffix –"logy" means a branch of learning, or study of a particular subject. In this case autology refers to the study of oneself. In essence you will be studying YOU!

One of the first times humans have been invited to study themselves was in ancient Greece when the Delphic maxim "Know Thyself" or "gnothi seauton" was inscribed in the pronaos (forecourt) of the Temple of Apollo, according to the Greek writer Pausanias. The aphorism is thought to have come from Luxor in Ancient Egypt, but has been used by many different philosophers and sages in a myriad of ways.

Autology, in the context of this book and the journey in which you are embarking upon, means to intimately know your own soul. There's a deeper part of you that has yet to be explored and expressed, and the journey of autology will indeed take you there.

Are You Prepared for This Journey?

As with any journey, it serves much better to be well prepared than not. There are a few things that you must have for your journey to be successful. Some of these are physical items, while others are attributes that you must invoke in order to navigate the terrain and overcome any obstacles. Here is what you will need:

Honesty — You will need complete honesty with yourself. This is listed first because it is the most important. Self-honesty is essential to self-understanding.

Courage — You will need courage to face yourself in a way that not many people are willing to do. As such, this may make for an uncomfortable journey at times.

Desire — One cannot be compelled by anyone else to take a journey this deep. One must have a desire from within.

Time & Space — You will need a quiet space for reflection and contemplation. You will need time to reflect and write your deepest thoughts; this should be done wholeheartedly and patiently.

A Journal or notebook — There are pages in this book designed to be used as a journal, but in the event that you would like to write more than the pages provided will allow or if you are reading this in ebook format, you can use a spiral or composition notebook or another personal journal.

A pen — Use a pen that you really enjoy writing with.

Curiosity — To get the most out of this journey, approach each question with curiosity as if you were a child filled with awe and wonder. Follow where each question leads you like a toddler following a butterfly.

Frequently Asked Questions

Is this book about spirituality?

This book is for those who feel compelled to know and live life from the inside out. Those of you who feel that there is something more to life than the relentless cycle of brushing your teeth, going to work, eating dinner, watching TV, going to bed, and... repeat. If you are drawn to this book then you probably have major questions that you'd like to have honest, clear answers to. Some of you may be distrustful, fearful, have an aversion to, or even a disdain for religion. I'm not going to try and deceive you: This book has serious undertones of spirituality and will quote religious texts that are applicable to the point that I'm trying to convey. Honestly, there really is more to you than the physical body that you're in. This guidebook, however, is about your learning how to find the answers to your deepest questions and my first promise to you is that I will not provide those answers. Not because I know something more and I want to keep information from you, but because I could never answer the questions you were born to live into.

Am I a guru or spiritual teacher?

I do not consider myself a guru or teacher, but more comparable to a midwife. Much like the metaphor that Socrates uses to describe his work, I seek to help others to give birth to the truth and wisdom that is divinely seeded within them. You can teach someone how to cook an omelet, you cannot teach someone about his or her own soul, and furthermore, even the omelet may not come out well. You already have an inner teacher that will guide you. My work is to guide you to your inner teacher. My second promise to you is that my inner teacher is guiding me in writing this book dedicated to divine truth, which is inclusive of your personal self-discovery and divine purpose.

Why did I write this book?

Self-inquiry is one of the greatest tools that lead to my spiritual awakening. I didn't call it self-inquiry at the time and I certainly didn't know that my own curiosity would lead to something so meaningful and profound. Some of the considerations in this book I asked myself as a kid. That is the time when our true questions about life and existence begins, but both fortunately and unfortunately those questions go unanswered. Mostly because the adults around us had not yet lived into their own answers. This is good, no one else's answers to your questions are of any absolute value to you.

My third promise to you is that the questions in this guided journal will begin to open space within you. It is imperative that you come before each question as child, humble and willing to learn, curious and full of wonder, sincere, honest, and without pretense.

This book is created from my own distance-less journey and connection to unitive life and that is truly all I ever have to offer. I have been on this journey for many years and I am still in awe of its beauty and mystique. This book is a love letter written especially for you in hopes that you are so enchanted by your own true nature that you follow it to freedom.

Are you ready to begin your journey?

Part I:

Truth, Existence, and the Soul

It is not the answer that enlightens,
but the question.

— Eugene Ionesco

Every Answer Begins
With a Question

Our inner journey begins when we are children. It begins with questions. Sometimes, these questions are voiced aloud and sometimes they are quietly contemplated. The first soul-stirring question I remember asking was one that was quietly contemplated. I remember exactly where I was when I asked myself this question. In the living room, to the right of me, was a high back striped sofa in earthy tones of tan, fawn and brown. It was the 70s. The fabric felt fibrous, both rough and soft, like tweed or wool, but I was not sitting on it – just standing near it and aware of its presence. I was standing in front of the TV, watching a commercial prompting viewers to give money to help starving children in Africa, Asia and Latin America. I was 5 or 6 years old, and some of the kids in the commercial were about the same age. My heart was broken for the very first time. Inside of the intense sadness that I felt was the question, "Why?" My mind raced to the image of my family's last meal. We weren't rich – by any means – but there was food to spare. We went to restaurants, and I rarely ate all the food available to me. There was always something on my plate to take home in a "doggy bag," which, even worse, was a term that implied that food was in such abundance that the left-over meal would be taken home and given to the family pet rather than feeding a starving human. I could not piece together how there could be a surfeit of food and drink available but only to some humans and not all. My sadness began to turn into anger. It was preposterous and stupid (I had just learned the word "preposterous"). I asked the adults in the room if we could bring some of the kids from the commercial to our home, and with pain in their eyes as well, their response was, "It's a little more complicated than that, baby."

Although I felt sad, angry and powerless in that moment, asking "why" opened up a space in me for further exploration into the deep pain that I felt. It was not the first question I'd ever asked, but it was the first time I'd ever questioned consensus reality, and it was definitely the first time I'd ever given adults the side-eye and wondered how they could let something like this happen to children. It was my first realization that perhaps our world was a little different than what I'd seen on Sesame Street and in Mr. Roger's Neighborhood. It was also the first time I remember my soul rising up in defense of another soul's dignity.

The innocence of unadorned curiosity must be present if we are to learn and grow at any age or during any stage in our lives.

✎

Find a quiet place to sit where you're not likely to be disturbed.

Take five slow, deep breaths and consider:

What are your most memorable childhood questions?

Where were you?

Who was there?

Did you ask the questions aloud or to yourself?

Did you receive an answer or are you still searching for an answer?

✎

What are your most memorable childhood questions?

Where were you and who was there when you asked your questions?

Did you ask the questions aloud or to yourself?

Did you receive an answer or are you still searching for an answer?

I wanna really, really, really wanna zig-a-zig ah.

— The Spice Girls

THE SPICE GIRLS

If you were anywhere on this planet in 1996 (or thereafter) then you have probably heard this song:

> Yo, I'll tell you what I want, what I really, really want
> So tell me what you want, what you really, really want
> I'll tell you what I want, what I really, really want
> So tell me what you want, what you really, really want
> I wanna, (ha) I wanna, (ha) I wanna, (ha) I wanna, (ha)
> I wanna really, really, really wanna zig-a-zig ah.

I'm smiling deeply as I write out the lyrics to this nonsensical song, not just because it is a fun song to recall, but because this particular song was profoundly instrumental in my journey of self-discovery. The name of the song is "Wannabe," and while listening to this song one day, I realized that the great irony of this song is that the singers never actually say what they "wanna be" and the only thing they really, really want is a "zig-a-zig ah," which, unfortunately, most folks have no clue as to what that is. Somehow, the out of keeping qualities of this song led me into a state of curiosity and wonder, and as the lyrics came around again ("So tell me what you want, what you really, really want"), my soul spoke, and I knew in an instant what it was that I really, really wanted.

Freedom, my soul said, "Freedom"

At the time (I was a young adult), my mind's idea of freedom was what most young adults living in western civilization would consider freedom to be. I remember thinking specifically, "I'd like to not have to wake up to an alarm clock; I'd like to have the time and money to pursue the things that I love to do and I'd like to not have to answer to anyone." Thirteen years passed before grace allowed me to see the true meaning of freedom from a soul perspective.

❦

Find a quiet place to sit where you're not likely to be disturbed.

Take five slow, deep breaths and consider:

What do you really want?

Write a detailed entry about your response.

How would you achieve it?

What must you say "no" to?

What must you say "yes" to?

❦

What do you really want?
Write a detailed entry about your response.

How would you achieve it?

What must you say "no" to?

What must you say "yes" to?

All things are in flux; the flux is subject to a unifying measure or rational principle. This principle (logos, the hidden harmony behind all change) bound opposites together in a unified tension, which is like that of a lyre, where a stable harmonious sound emerges from the tension of the opposing forces that arise from the bow bound together by the string.

— Heraclitus

We can speak and think only of what exists. And what exists is uncreated and imperishable for it is whole and unchanging and complete. It was not or nor shall be different since it is now, all at once, one and continuous...

— Parmenides

BEING AND BECOMING /
THE CHANGING AND
THE UNCHANGING

Heraclitus, one of the more obscure pre-Socratic philosophers, is best known for his doctrine on change being central to existence. His most famous aphorisms (loosely translated) include: "No man ever steps into the same river twice," and "The only thing that is constant is change." In Ancient Greece, there was a saying attributed to Heraclitus, "Panta rhei." In Greek, panta rhei means 'everything flows.' Heraclitus believed that the world, and everything in it, is in constant flux. His analogy of our world being a river has been thought to mean that not only is a river constantly changing due to the swiftness and speed of the flowing water, but also because we humans are constantly evolving and changing from moment to moment. Heraclitus also likened the underlying nature of our world to fire because of its ever-changing nature and its ability to destroy and transform. Heraclitus believed in the cyclic recurrence of all things.

Another pre-Socratic philosopher, named Parmenides, thought to be the father of Metaphysics, had what some have deemed as opposing ideas about the universe and existence. Parmenides' doctrine holds that nothing ever changes - there is no coming into existence, nor ceasing to exist. He asserts that existence is eternal and immobile and that change is only an illusion. In the endless philosophical debate on being versus becoming, Parmenides was most interested in the truth behind "dóxa" a Greek word that has many meanings, such as: opinions, appearances, judgments, expectations and beliefs. Parmenides believed that becoming and change were merely appearances and that true "being" is timeless and unchanging.

In summary, Heraclitus believed that the world is in constant change, and that as a consequence of perpetual change, knowledge is also ever-changing. While on the other hand, Parmenides believed that there is no change and, ultimately, there is no movement, therefore the only way to understand knowledge is by way of truth, which is always the same and never changing.

❧

Find a quiet place to sit where you're not likely to be disturbed.

What do you feel?

Take five slow deep breaths and consider:

Is there an ever-changing nature within me? Describe it.

Is there something in me or about me that never changes? Describe it.

Am I being, becoming, both, or neither? Write about it.

What unanswered questions do I have about existence, being or becoming?

❧

Is there an ever-changing nature within me? Describe it.

Is there something in me or about me that never changes?
Describe it.

Am I being, becoming, both, or neither? Write about it.

What unanswered questions do I have about existence, being or becoming?

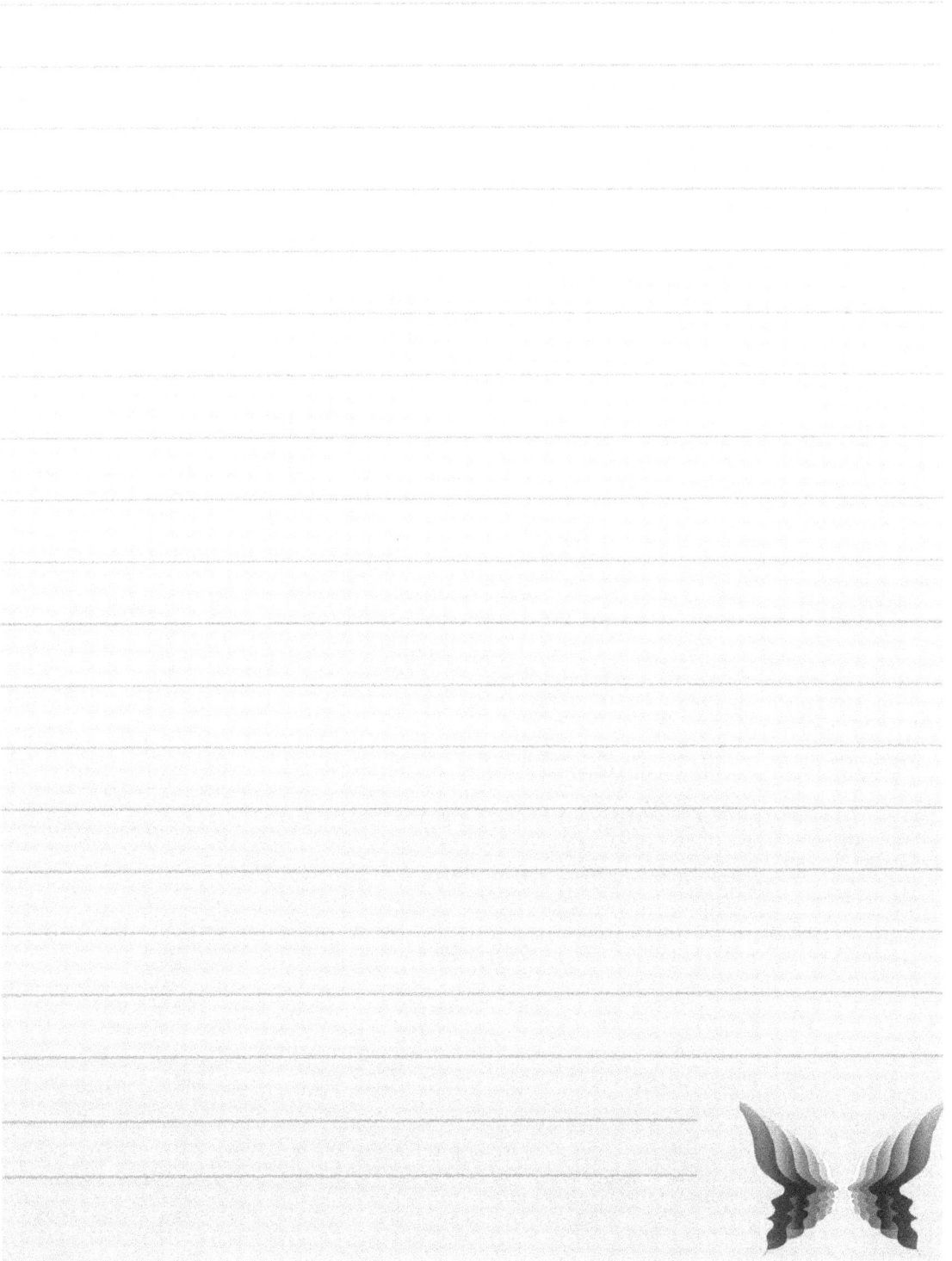

I believe that truth has only one face:
  that of a violent contradiction.

— Georges Bataille

Finding Truth
in Contradictions

One of the things that makes finding truth so difficult are the contradictions we find in everyday living. Even our supposedly wise proverbs contradict each other. For instance, have you ever wondered if "Opposites attract" or do "Birds of a feather flock together?" Do our "actions speak louder than words" or is it that "the pen is mightier than the sword?" Are we "Better safe than sorry" or do we take a risk thinking, "Nothing ventured, nothing gained?"

We are told that it is kind to be selfless and put the needs of others first. We are also told that if we do not take care of our own needs first, we cannot tend to the needs of others properly. We are advised to love ourselves as we are, and we are also told to be the best that we can be. Is it okay to give money to a person asking on the street, or will that make us partially responsible for their ruin if they are drug addicts or alcoholics?

❦

Find a quiet place to sit where you're not likely to be disturbed.
Take five slow deep breaths and consider:

What are the contradictions in life that you think about most often? What is true of each conflicting perspective? What do you disagree with and why?

In a world of contradictions, how do you make the right decisions? How do you know what is true?

❦

What are the contradictions in life
that you think about most often?

What is true of each conflicting perspective?
What do you disagree with and why?

In a world of contradictions, how do you make the right decisions?
How do you know what is true?

There is an old illusion – it is called good and evil.

— Friedrich Nietzsche

The Thief, The Old Lady, and the Friendly Neighbor

A thief plots to break into an old woman's house on a Sunday morning, a time when he knows she's always at church. One Sunday he creeps up to her back window and smashes it with a hammer. After he looks inside, he sees that the old woman is not at church – she is in there, lying face down on the floor. The sight of the body scares the burglar and he runs away; he wanted to commit a burglary, but being arrested for murder was not a part of his plan. But what the burglar did not know was that the old woman was not dead, she was unconscious, having passed out because of a carbon monoxide leak that would have killed her. When the burglar broke the window, he let out some of the toxic gas and let in fresh air which allowed her to regain consciousness.

Imagine the same premises as the above scenario, but in this case the "thief" is just a friendly neighbor who makes it a point to say hello to the old woman every morning. When the old lady didn't answer the door the neighbor decided to look in the window. The neighbor sees the old woman's body on the floor and breaks in to try to resuscitate her while help is on its way. In his panic, he accidentally applied too much force and crushed her ribs, causing multiple internal hemorrhages and eventually death. What he did not know was that the woman had passed out due to a carbon monoxide leak, and would have been fine had he left her alone and waited for the paramedics to arrive.

Metaethics is an examination of what we mean when we use ethical language. When we make ethical judgments or claims that something or someone is either good or bad, right or wrong.

❧

Find a quiet place to sit where you're not likely to be disturbed.

Take five slow deep breaths and consider:

> **How do you know when something is truly right or wrong? What informs your own ethics/morality?**
>
> **Do moral facts exist?**
>
> **Write about something that you thought was bad but turned out to be good or something you thought was good that turned out to be bad.**

❧

How do you know when something is truly right or wrong?

What informs your own ethics/morality?

Do moral facts exist?

Write about something that you thought was bad but turned out to be good or something you thought was good that turned out to be bad.

It is spring again.
The earth is like a child that knows poems by heart.

— Rainer Maria Rilke

What Is This Place

I've heard earth referred to as many different things to many different people. Over centuries people have formed a plethora of ideas about this planet and life upon it. Some people refer to earth as their home, while others think of earth as a school where our souls comes to learn and mature. I've also heard that earth is a prison that we are trapped in, a playground that we just came to play around on, oh, and I've also heard that earth is hell (not just a difficult planet to live on, but the actual "hell"). Movies have suggested that we live in a socio-economic simulation or "Matrix" and some religions view life on earth as Maya, meaning "an illusion or dream." There are those who view life as a video game with different levels to overcome, and let's not forget the people who think the earth is flat. What do you think?

❧

Find a quiet place to sit where you're not likely to be disturbed.

Take five slow deep breaths and consider:

What is planet earth to you?

Does life exist only on earth, or does life exist on other planets as well?

Write about the weirdest or most interesting idea you've ever heard about earth?

❧

What is planet earth to you?

Does life exist only on earth, or does life exist
on other planets as well?

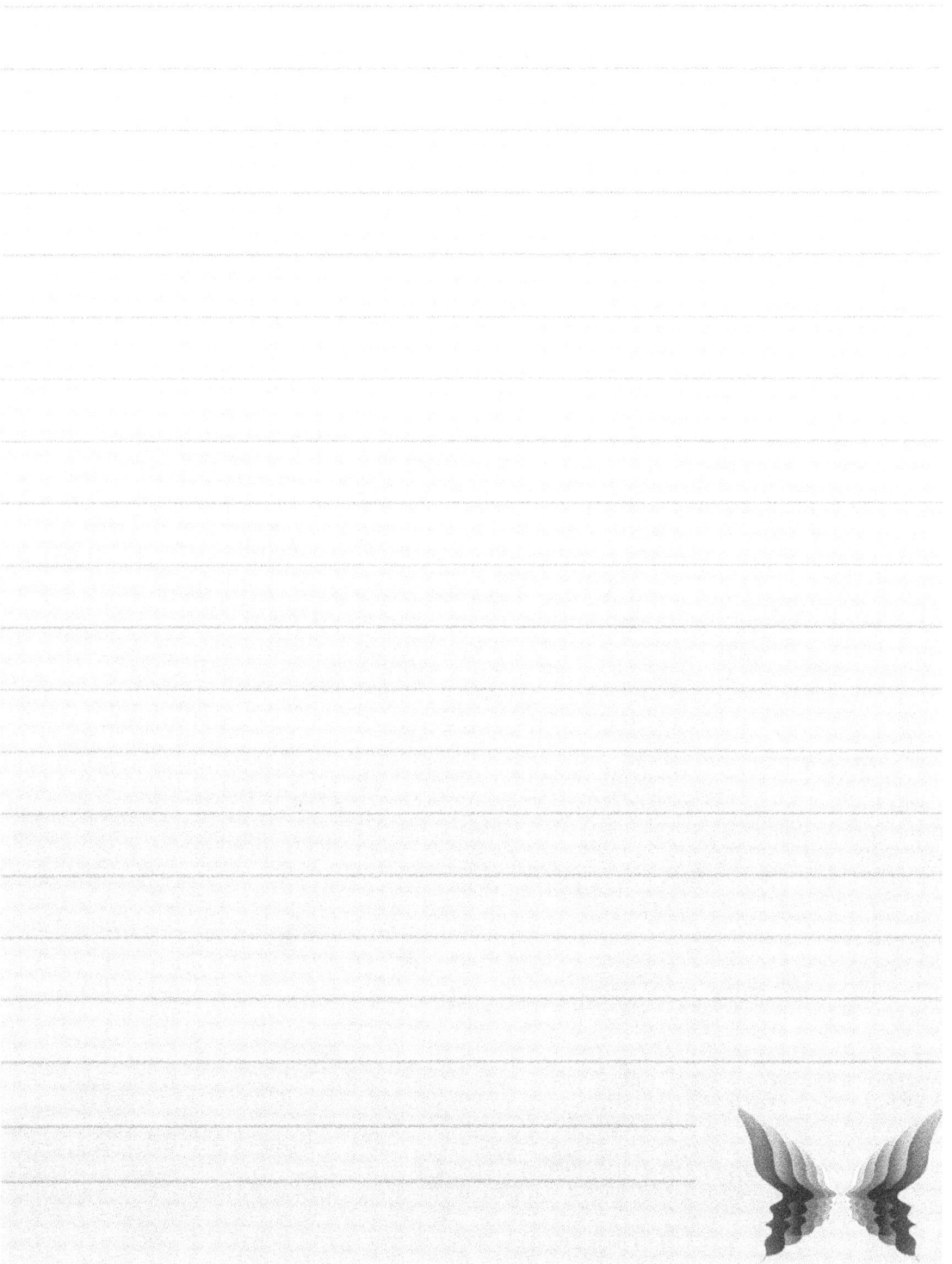

Write about the weirdest or most interesting idea
you've ever heard about earth?

TOOLBOX FOR TRUTH, EXISTENCE, AND THE SOUL

Generally when we think of truth, we are thinking of relative truth, a truth that is dependent upon the perception of an object. Relative truth relates to how things exist. Absolute truth is the nature of exstence or existence itself. Religion, philosophy, spirituality, and autology are all methods that seek absolute truth. When someone says that they are speaking *their truth* it is always a relative truth. Absolute truth includes everyone and belongs to no one.

Here is what truth looks like from the perspective of relative truth, and from absolute truth:

Relative Truth	Absolute Truth
Knowledge	Knowing
An infinite number of truths / perceptions	Always One
An infinite number of oppositions	Has no opposites
Conditioned by time and space	Unconditional
How things exist	Existence itself
Exclusive	Inclusive
Conceptual	Beyond concepts/filters
Data / Information	Wisdom
Can breed uncertainty	Clarity
May only be true for one or a portion of society	Is true for all, all of the time
Is linear / logical	Is non-linear / Spontaneous
Is acquired	Is revealed

Part II:

THE BATTLE WITHIN

The supreme art of war is to subdue the enemy without fighting.

— Sun Tzu

LUKE, DARTH AND YODA

I was 13 when I first noticed it. Sitting on my twin sized bed, back against the wall, curious but solemn, I muttered to myself, "There's a battle going on inside of me." Although quite shocked at the words that had just come from my mouth, there was no sense of exigency, nor vexation, nor was there fear. I do, however, remember a feeling of discomfort, a heaviness from within. The heaviness one might feel setting upon a daunting task. Though I was only 13, I knew that moment of realization to be profound, even if I didn't quite understand why. That was the day that I became aware of the inner push and pull that goes on inside of all of us. I call it, "The day Luke Skywalker met Darth Vader while Yoda sat quietly behind a curtain, observing the whole thing." We don't learn about this inner battle growing up in our homes, it's not talked about around the dinner table nor is it taught in school. Even in church, this topic is not discussed in terms of the depth and breadth of one's own experience of it. Honestly, years later, I am still in awe of the grace that allowed me to notice the subtle feelings of disunity inside. I never told anyone about my inner conflict. I wasn't quite sure if the whole thing was normal or not, and me, being a dawning teenager, wanted very much to appear as normal as possible. At least normal enough to not say, "Hey Mom, Luke Skywalker and Darth Vader are fighting in me!" I believe that it was this time in my life that marked the beginning of my interest in self-inquiry and self-discovery. My questioning of this inner battle is how the vehicle of autology began to carry me along this path.

In Judaism, the battle that I speak of is said to be between the yetzer hara, the so-called inclination to do evil, and the yetzer hatov, the so-called inclination to do good. In most rabbinic literature, the yetzer hara is not an evil or demonic force per se, but rather, man's misuse of the natural urges that guide us toward survival. For instance, our need to eat in order to sustain life can turn into gluttony because of the yetzer hara and our desire to share love, intimacy, and pleasure with another person can become a lust that drives only personal satisfaction due to this inclination. If we look probingly into modern-day society, it's pretty easy to find examples of this. Our most basic desires to have our needs met have, to a large degree, turned into over-indulgence, pleasure seeking and avarice.

According to the *Avot d'Rabbi Natan* (a guide on how to study the *Torah*), everyone is born with a yetzer hara, but the yetzer hatov enters a child at around the age of 12 or 13, which oddly enough, happened to be around the age that I became aware of the inner battle.

The yetzer hara sounds a lot like what is known in both spiritual and psychological circles as the ego, or the lower self (I use the term conceptual self); that which inspires service only to one's own personal sense of self, and the yetzer hatov can be likened to the Holy Spirit, Christ-consciousness, Buddha-nature or the higher self; that which inspires service to the unitive life. Regardless of what we call these two forces, it is the pulling in opposite directions of these two poles within us that causes the majority of not only our personal suffering, but also our collective suffering as humanity.

This inner battle takes on many forms, and along this path of self-inquiry, it is important to become aware of our own inner landscape and the battles that ensue upon it. In order to gain a better understanding of how the yetzer hara gains power and influence in our psyche, we have to first see the division of power within ourselves. There are many ways of perceiving within each of us. One way of perceiving is through the vision of our conceptual self, and another way of seeing is with our soul.

❧

Find a quiet place where you're not likely to be disturbed.

Take five slow, deep breaths and consider:

The battle within is a part of the human condition.

> **Can you sense the battle within you? What does it feel like?**

> **When did you first notice it? Is the battle for or against someone or something?**

❧

Can you sense the battle within you?
What does it feel like?

When did you first notice it?
Is the battle for or against someone or something?

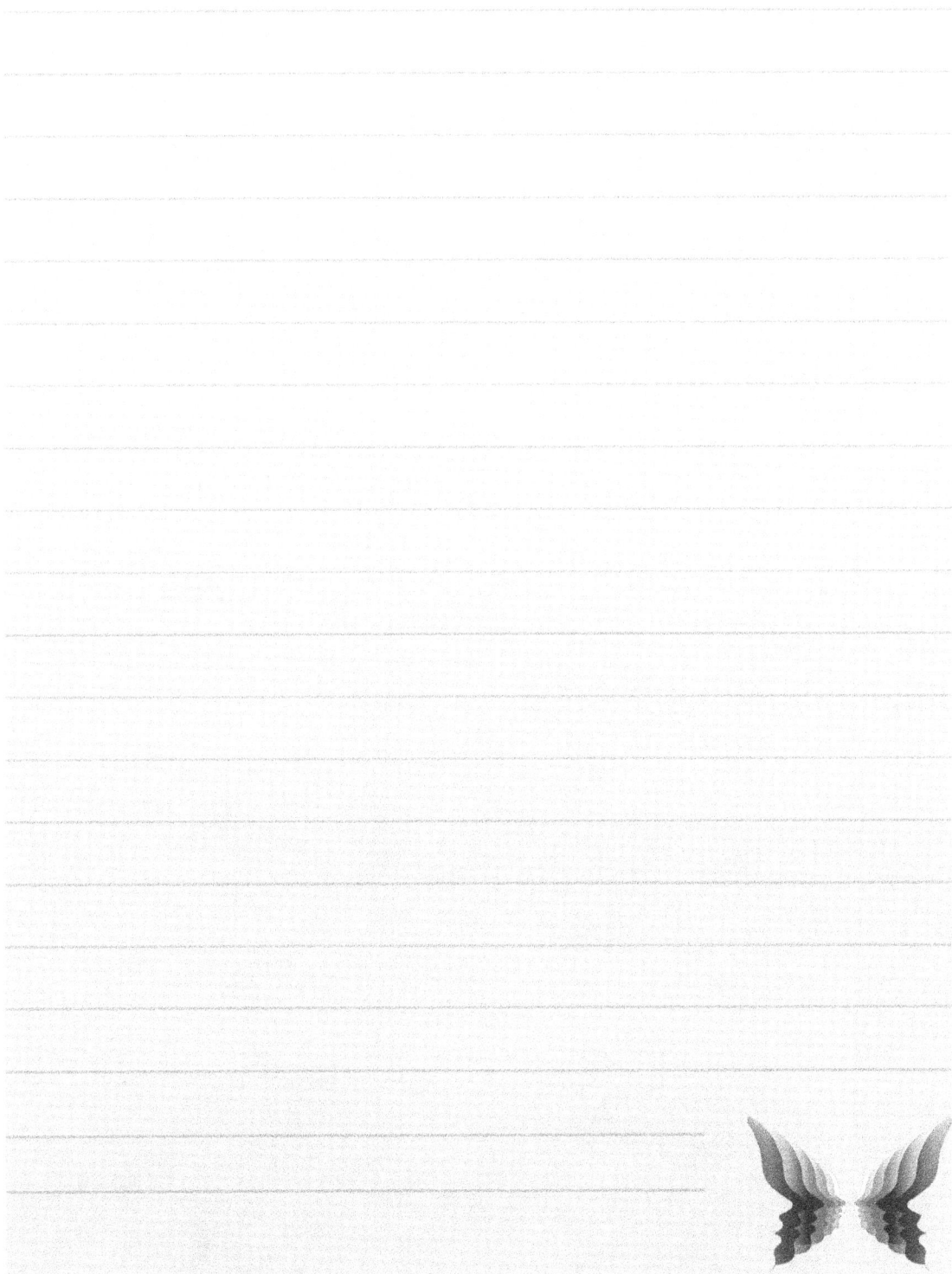

Be yourself—not your idea of what you think somebody else's idea of yourself should be.

— Henry David Thoreau

THE LOOKING GLASS SELF

Another aspect of the conceptual self is the looking-glass self. The looking-glass self was first introduced by Charles Horton Cooley in 1902 in his work, *Human Nature and the Social Order*. The looking-glass self theory asserts that our behavior, and how we view ourselves, is based on how we believe others view us. The looking-glass self comprises three main components that are unique to humans (Shaffer 2005).

1. We imagine how we must appear to others in a social situation.
2. We imagine and react to what we feel their judgment of that appearance must be.
3. We develop our sense of self and respond through the perceived judgments of others.

The basic concept is that humans use other humans as a mirror—or looking-glass—to see a reflection of who they are so that they may adjust their behavior accordingly. We have all learned to do this, being the social creatures that we are. A common example of how we use the looking-glass self in everyday life would be simply walking into a room. We notice the expressions on people's faces. Are they happy to see us, or do they look uncomfortable and avoid eye contact? Another example is when we seek the attention of someone to whom we'd like to be closer and follow their cues and adjust our behavior according to what we think is favorable to them.

This way of interacting also appears to be a natural and normal way of communicating and relating with others, but it bears the distortion of inauthenticity and is a hindrance to one's true expression. The looking-glass self is highly changeable and unstable, since it is an identity based on one's perception of other people's views, regardless of whether that perception is accurate and, most importantly, whether or not the communication is issuing from the authority of the other person's true self or the distortion of the conceptual-self.

❧

Find a quiet place to sit where you're not likely to be disturbed.

Take five slow, deep breaths and consider:

Imagine yourself walking into a room with other people.

What kind of presence do you bring when you walk into a room filled with people?

Do you bring that same type of presence into an empty room?   How do you know?

❧

What kind of presence do you bring when you
walk into a room filled with people?

Do you bring that same type of presence
into an empty room? How do you know?

If you are always trying to be normal,
you will never know how amazing you can be.

— Maya Angelou

THE TRIBAL SELF

There are many moving parts that make up the conceptual self. One of those parts is called "the tribal self," which is the part of the conceptual self that connects us to those with whom we are most comfortable and familiar, like our family and friends. When we were children, we learned the ways of our family members and assimilated their behaviors, morals and values into our own lives. It was such a seamless process we never even thought twice about it. In fact, we just called it "growing up." We took on the beliefs, struggles and pride of the tribe. It was all we knew. While we were growing up, our mom, dad, grandparents, aunts, uncles, older siblings, teachers and friends were forming our conceptual self. Also being integrated, were ideas and concepts about our gender and the "other" gender, our religion and the "other" religions, our sports teams and the "other" teams, our race and the "other" races, our political party, the "other" political party and tribal pride began to take root. Our tribal self is responsible for the production of our most primal psychological responses, and those responses usually portray the tribe as being right, or superior, and anyone who disagrees with the tribe as being wrong, or inferior. It seems natural and harmless for the adults in the family to pass knowledge and traditions down to the next generation, but when that knowledge is only passed down through the perspective of the tribal or conceptual self, a distortion is assimilated and perpetuated from generation to generation.

As we grow in spiritual maturity and move closer to our own true nature, we begin to question tribal ideologies. We wonder if the familiar concepts and traditions that we've held so dear should be common consuetude in our own lives as well as the lives of present and future generations.

❧

Find a quiet place to sit where you're not likely to be disturbed.

Take five slow, deep breaths and consider:

What are the tribal beliefs that I hold dear?

What are the tribal beliefs that I question?

Who am I without tribal beliefs?

❧

What are the tribal beliefs that I hold dear?

What are the tribal beliefs that I question?

Who am I without tribal beliefs?

I learned to be with myself rather than avoiding myself with limiting habits; I started to be aware of my feelings more, rather than numb them.

— Judith Wright

BAD HABITS AND ADDICTION

Bad habits and addictions are topics about which most of us would rather not talk. In Autology, it is imperative that we face the issues that keep us in misalignment to our own true nature. An addiction is when a person uses substances, or engages in behaviors that become habitual and uncontrollable - despite harmful and destructive consequences. A person can be addicted to substances and behaviors such as drugs, alcohol, sugar, caffeine, shopping, social media, food, nicotine, pain, shoplifting, sex, gambling and more. Addiction can make you feel as though you are trapped in a cycle of physical, mental and spiritual torment without any way to escape. If this sounds like you, Dear Heart, do not be dismayed. I stand with you as you face your addiction and find the true nature within you that is not addicted or dependent upon any substance or behavior. It is time to face your shadows as you consider the questions below. In the toolbox on pp. 97-99 are resources to help you along this journey.

In the toolbox on pp. 97-99 are resources to help you along this journey.

❦

Find a quiet place to sit where you're not likely to be disturbed.

Take five slow, deep breaths and...

Consider:

All addictions and compulsions are distractions from painful emotions.

Make a list of your bad habits and addictions.

What is the source of your pain? Write it out.

In what ways do your bad habits/addictions keep you from living the life that you want to live?

What lies do you tell yourself in order to continue your bad habits/addictions?

Who are the people you must remove yourself from to break your bad habits/addictions?

Who are the people you can rely on to help you overcome your bad habits/addictions?

Write a letter of compassion to your addicted self (write a letter to yourself as if you were a loving friend who understands your addiction).

Write a letter of encouragement to yourself from your future self who has overcome this addiction (how would your future-self encourage you to overcome your bad habits/addictions?).

Make a list of your bad habits and addictions.

What is the source of your pain? Write it out.

In what ways do your bad habits/addictions keep you from living the life that you want to live?

What lies do you tell yourself in order to continue your
bad habits/addictions?

Who are the people you must remove yourself from to break your bad habits/addictions?

Who are the people you can rely on to help you overcome your bad habits/addictions?

Write a letter of compassion to your addicted self (write a letter to yourself as if you were a loving friend who understands your addiction).

Write a letter of encouragement to yourself from your future self who has overcome this addiction (how would your future-self encourage you to overcome your bad habits/addictions?).

TOOLBOX FOR THE BATTLE WITHIN

This chart can be used a guide to help you understand when your thoughts and actions are sourced from love (the true self) or from fear (ego or the constructed self). Begin to notice the space that exists before any thought or action, within that space is your power to choose your source: **Love or fear.**

THE TRUE SELF	THE CONSTRUCTED SELF
Love	Fear
Authentic in speech and action	Concerned with how one is perceived
Fresh and spontaneous	Plans, Conspires and Rehearses
Accepting of self and others	Critical of self and others
Does not hold tightly to identity, and does not recognize others as an identity	Holds tightly to identity and works to prove its identity to self and others
Gives and receives graciously	Likes to receive but withholds giving due to fear of being used or taken advantage of
Feels feelings spontaneously including anger, Is okay with vulnerability	Hides or denies feelings, carries resentment, Is aggressive and/or overly passive
Open to intuition, uses wisdom primarily and logic secondarily	Methodical, uses only logical thinking to solve problems
Childlike	Childish
Seeks to break free of unhealthy patterns	Acts out painful patterns repeatedly
Is a vessel for Divine power	Seeks external power only (external power is any power that can be taken away)
Self-Aware	Self-Absorbed
Detached from outcomes	Attached to outcomes
Seeks to reveal and express the inner world	Is constantly rearranging the outer world
Private self	Public self
Oneness	Separation
Acts in honesty and integrity	Will make exceptions regarding being honest and in integrity to benefit one's own causes
Perpetuates healing	Perpetuates suffering
Seeks for truth in self and others	Seeks one upmanship over others (engaging in gossip, judging and/or thinking oneself as better or morally superior)

Tool for Forgiveness of Self and Others:

Ho'oponopono

The Hawaiian word ho'oponopono is made up of two parts, ho'o ("to make") and pono ("right"). The word pono is repeated to indicate "making right" not only with another person, but also "making right" with oneself. In short, ho'opono-pono means to forgive. It is a cleansing tool that removes the toxicity of fear and doubt from your mind and replaces it with forgiveness and gratitude. It also helps us take 100% responsibility for every negative perception and experience that comes into our lives and helps us discover the Divinity within. When you are having negative thoughts and you can't turn them off, or when someone comes up to you and wants to gossip, or when you feel fear or pain because you or someone you know is suffering, repeat the ho'oponopono mantra (in any order):

I'm sorry
Please forgive me
Thank you
I love you

US Help Hotlines

If you or someone you know needs immediate help for an addiction please call the appropriate number below. A simple phone call could change your life.

General Drug Addiction Hotlines:
SAMHSA (government/tax sponsored): 1-800-622-4357
Ecstasy Addiction: 1-800-468-6933
Alcohol Treatment Referral Hotline: 1-800-252-6465 (24 hours)
Cocaine Hotline: 1-800-262-2463 (24 hours)

Christian/Religious-Based
Alcoholics for Christ: 1-800-441-7877

Sex Addiction
Project Know: 1-888-892-1840
Sex Addicts Anonymous: 1-800-477-8191

Gambling Addiction
Compulsive Gambling Hotline: 1-410-332-0402
National Problem Gambling Hotline: 1-800-522-4700

Food Addiction
Overeaters Anonymous: 1-505-891-2664
National Eating Disorders: 1-800-931-2237
Food Addicts Anonymous: 772-878-9657

Video Game & Internet Addiction
Computer Gaming Addicts Anonymous: 970-364-3497

Youth/Children

National Association for Children of Alcoholics: 1-888-554-2627

National Youth Crisis Hotline: 1-800-448-4663

Provides 24/7 short-term counseling and referrals to local drug treatment centers, shelters, and counseling services. Responds to youth dealing with pregnancy, molestation, suicide, and child abuse.

Children of Alcoholics Foundation: 1-800-359-2623

12-Step Programs

Families Anonymous: 1-800-736-9805

Narcotics Anonymous 1-818-773-9999

Cocaine Anonymous 1-310-559-5833

Crystal Meth Anonymous: 1-855-METH-FREE

Marijuana Anonymous: 1-800-766-6779

Nicotine Anonymous: 1-877-879-6422

Nar-Anon: (800) 477-6291

(Monday – Friday | 9AM – 5PM PST)

Narcotics Anonymous: 1-818-773-9999

Alcoholics Anonymous: 510-839-8900

(East Bay, CA, but should work for anyone – 24 hours)

Part III:

THE CREATOR'S GIFT

*It is more important to be of pure intention
than of perfect action.*

— Ilyas Kassam

Tools and Intention

We are a bit like the characters in a Harry Potter book, innocently bumbling about, trying to learn how to make magic happen. We start off as greenhorns, much like Potter at the beginning of his journey. He was unaware of his own ability to create magic. In the beginning, he created situations haphazardly out of fear or anger; situations that he didn't even know that he was creating. Much like in our lives, it seemed as if things were "just happening." This is where we all begin, unaware of our own power. Autology is about your willingness to take a look at what and how you are creating, in every moment. To be more specific, it is about examining and gaining an understanding of the cause and effect of your own creating, while also developing an astute awareness into how suffering is created unintentionally so that you may master the art of creating from a space that is authentic and wholehearted. What is authentic and wholehearted for you can never turn out to be wrong or cause suffering for anyone else.

As you learn to master creating with authenticity and wholehearted intention, it is helpful to become aware of the vast array of tools at hand for both learning and creating. The tools available to each and every creator is...just about everything. There is nothing that you cannot use in order to learn, grow and create on this planet, with the exception of other sentient beings who have their own power of intention. Still, one can learn, grow and create in relation to others - that is what relationship is in its truest form. Much of the suffering in our world is caused by people using other people for personal pleasure and gain. What we do flows from who we are. If we do not know our true nature, and are not acting from a space of authentic power, what we create will undoubtedly be a product or situation made up of our fears, skewed perceptions, blind acceptance of someone else's worldview or a shuddersome combination of the three. Becoming aware of the intention behind every action, or non-action, is the beginning of true self-mastery.

Allow me to show you how powerful a creator you are. Think of any object. You, as a creator, are the one that gives value and purpose to the object that you have just brought to mind, and your intention becomes the driving force behind whatever situation you create with that object. The object itself is always neutral; it is your intention as a creator that gives meaning to the experience that is created. Let's use a knife as an example. A knife is a neutral object created to cut things. Depending upon the intention of the user, it can either be used to hurt someone out of anger or vengeance or it can be used to free an animal that has accidentally trapped itself in netting. Or, how about a carton of eggs? You can use the eggs to make breakfast for your family, or you can throw them at an annoying neighbor's house in the middle of the night (don't do that). My point is, it is you who must become aware of what you bring to life. What needs to be examined is the dissonance between what we say our intentions are versus what our actions are. You will notice that as you become more and more aware of your own intentions, a sense of responsibility will naturally set in. Responsibility always follows awareness; one can't feel a proper sense of responsibility for his/her creations if he/she is unaware that it was he/she who created them. Being aware and taking full ownership over what we create allows the soul to be in its rightful position as master over the ego/conceptual self and as a more clear vessel and servant of the Divine.

Find a quiet place to sit where you're not likely to be disturbed.
Take five slow, deep breaths and consider:

Write about the last situation that you created unintentionally.

Looking back, what were the tools available to you?

How would the situation look if you created it with authentic and wholehearted intention?

What will you create today?

What tools will you use?

Write about the last situation that you created unintentionally.

Looking back, what were the tools available to you?

How would the situation look if you created it with authentic and wholehearted intention?

What will you create today?

What tools will you use?

Rule of thumb: The more important a call or action is to our soul's evolution, the more Resistance we will feel toward pursuing it.

— Steven Pressfield

RESISTANCE

Sometimes, when I sit down to write, I'm "in the flow," or "in the zone," meaning ideas are coming to me easily; I'm not struggling to find the perfect words to convey my thoughts, and time feels as though it doesn't even exist. But, then there are times when I sit down at my computer, and the voice in my head immediately begins its shenanigans: "A milkshake sure would be nice right now," or if that doesn't work, it gets more serious: "Did you forget to start the dryer? Go check to make sure." Not once have I gone to check the dryer and found that I'd forgotten to start it. Not once. If you are an artist, athlete, writer, musician or even if you just seek to do something good for yourself - like quitting smoking, eating healthier, beginning an exercise regimen or anything that requires even the least bit of discipline - you'll soon notice that there is a force that pushes against your efforts and dangles the most enticing temptations before you to steal away your attention and to distract you. *The War of Art* author, Steven Pressfield, calls this force "Resistance" (with a capital R). Resistance never shows up to stop you from eating too much pizza or from having one too many drinks. No, it only shows up to keep you from doing something that might make your life better. I've always been fascinated by this phenomenon, why it exists and why it's so darn effective. It is, of course, a force that can be overcome or people would never get anything done and the page that you're reading right now would be blank, because I'd be somewhere having a milkshake and watching Netflix instead of writing. Pressfield describes Resistance as "protean," meaning that it is able to take on any form. It can seduce you with fear, desire or what seems like completely logical reasoning - all to keep you from the task at hand. As you continue your journey of Autology, Resistance is an internal antagonist worth examining.

❧

Find a quiet place to sit where you're not likely to be disturbed.

Take five slow, deep breaths and consider:

Are you familiar with the force of Resistance? How does Resistance present itself to you?

What has Resistance tried to keep you from accomplishing? In what ways was Resistance successful?

Can you use Resistance in a way that is helpful?

❧

Are you familiar with the force of Resistance?
How does Resistance present itself to you?

What has Resistance tried to keep you from accomplishing?

In what ways was Resistance successful?

Can you use Resistance in a way that is helpful?

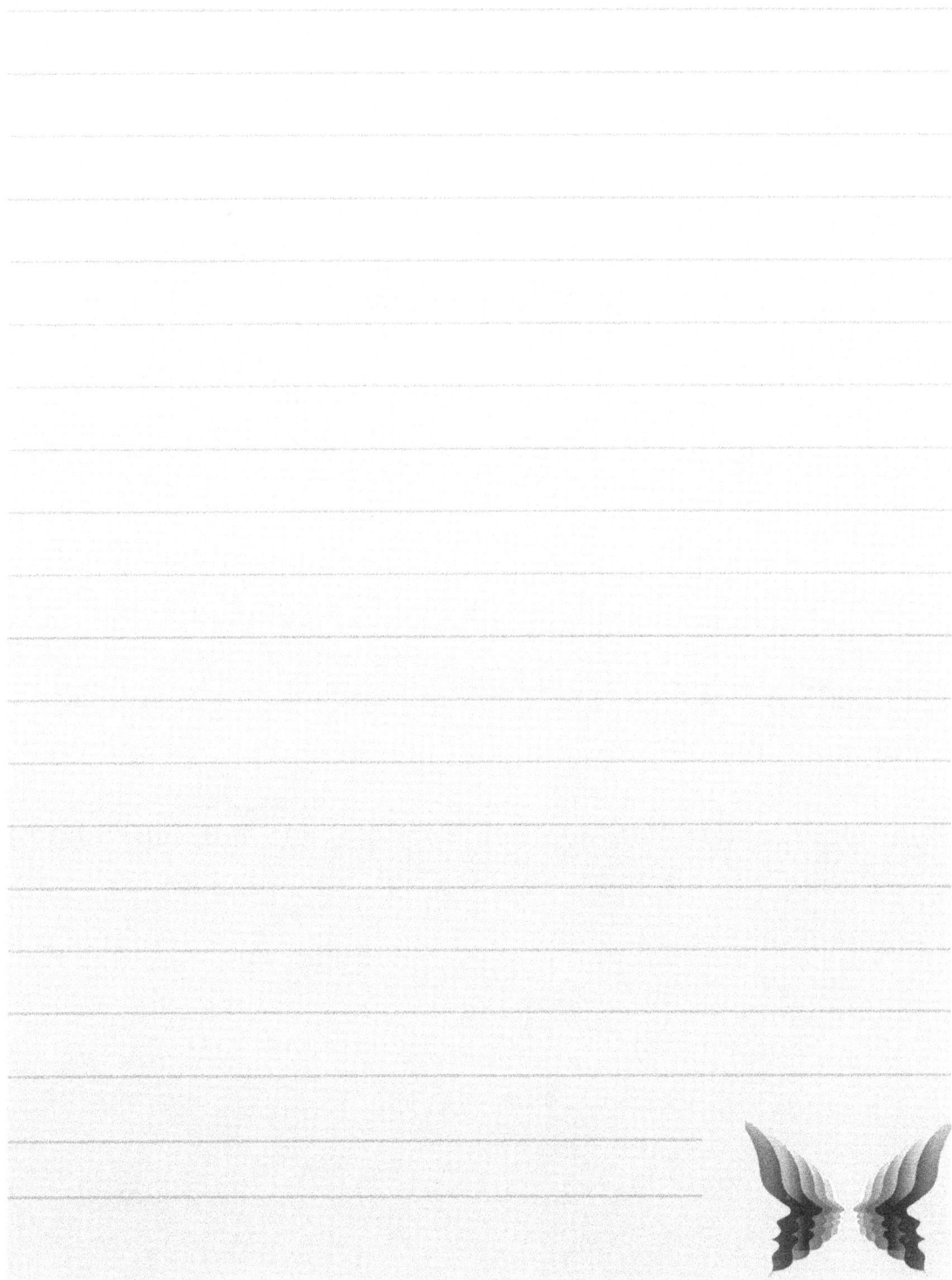

The body never lies.

— Martha Graham

INTUITIVE EATING

When you become quiet and mindful while eating, you will be able to feel the way food affects your body. Even now, there is information stored in your memory about how certain foods affect you physically and mentally. Intuitive eating is about getting in touch with your body's natural intelligence and allowing your body's sensations to inform your choices regarding hunger, food, and satiety. Remember, you're the expert when it comes to knowing what foods are best for your body, whether those foods should be eaten cooked or raw, and what times of the day are best to eat your meals. Trust yourself.

❧

Find a quiet place to sit where you're not likely to be disturbed.

Take five slow, deep breaths and consider:

What is your body telling you now regarding food? Are you hungry, full, satisfied, or overly full?

What foods affect you mentally (makes you jittery, mentally sluggish, etc.)?

List the foods that your body disagrees with?

What foods do you continue to eat despite your body sending you signals that you shouldn't?

What foods are you allergic to?

List the foods that make you feel good/healthy inside?

What signals does your body give you when it's hungry?

How do you know when you are full? What are the sensations you feel?

What is the best time of day for you to eat? Why?

What is your body telling you now regarding food?
Are you hungry, full, satisfied, or overly full?

What foods affect you mentally
(makes you jittery, mentally sluggish, etc.)?

List the foods that your body disagrees with?

What foods do you continue to eat despite your body
sending you signals that you shouldn't?

What foods are you allergic to?

List the foods that make you feel good/healthy inside?

What signals does your body give you when it's hungry?

How do you know when you are full?
What are the sensations you feel?

What is the best time of day for you to eat? Why?

I don't believe in astrology;
I'm a Sagittarius and we're skeptical.

— Arthur C. Clarke

THE STARS AND THE ELEMENTS

Many people say that they do not believe in astrology, but they maybe kinda notice that their dad, aunt and best friend all have similar traits and, coincidentally, were all born a few days apart in the month of April. Is this just a coincidence? I mentioned astrology to a friend once, and she immediately associated it with the devil. While I don't agree with her assessment of astrology, I do understand why she feels this way. Astrology is a tool that has been misused. Like nearly everything in modern society, it has been used as a means to an end and is thereby not being used for the highest good or at its fullest potential. Astrology was not originally intended as a tool for individual divination (fortune-telling and the like) but was considered an early science and gave birth to the science of Astronomy. As mentioned before, everything (with the exception of other sentient beings) is a creator's tool, and every tool can be used for the good - or for the detriment - of all. It's not the tool that holds meaning - it's the intention of the tool's user. The tool of Astrology is no exception. In Autology, Astrology can be used as a guide to help understand the challenging and liberating aspects of one's true nature.

Although I am not an astrologer, I do believe that there is a divine order to the universe, and that not only do celestial bodies have a role in our experiential existence, they are directly connected to our evolutionary progression/stagnation and spiritual maturity. Esoteric astrology is about the journey of the soul and is focused on the soul's purpose and what we contribute to the whole. The type of astrology that most people are used to seeing is exoteric, an astrology based solely on personality and the material world. Esoteric astrology can be very helpful in self-inquiry when its role is viewed in proper perspective, as a tool to discover how we, the individual puzzle piece, fits into the whole puzzle.

In the toolbox of this section (pp. 146-149) is a table that will allow you to find your zodiac sign, element, modality, both the challenging and liberating characteristics of each sign and the life lesson associated with that sign. Do not see the characteristics as something you *should* have, but rather as traits you either embody, desire to embody, or desire to transcend. This is a simple chart to begin self-inquiry, esoteric astrology is a lot more complicated than just looking at your sun sign and if you are interested in becoming more familiar with esoteric astrology I would suggest that you find material written by Alice A. Bailey or material from the Theosophical Society.

⊗

Find a quiet place to sit where you're not likely to be disturbed.

Take five slow deep breaths and consider:

Is there truth to any of the characteristics that are associated with your zodiac sign?
(See chart on pp. 148-149.)

What is true?

Which traits do you embody?

Which traits do you wish to be free of?

Which traits do you desire to develop?

Write from your heart about your astrological sign, liberating & challenging characteristics or element.

⊗

Is there truth to any of the characteristics that are associated
with your zodiac sign? What is true?

Which traits do you embody?

Which traits do you wish to be free of?

Which traits do you desire to develop?

Write from your heart about your astrological sign,
liberating & challenging characteristics or element.

Nothing in nature lives for itself. Rivers don't drink their own water. Trees don't eat their own fruit. Sun doesn't give heat for itself. Flowers don't spread fragrance for themselves.
Living for others is the rule of nature.
And therein lies the secret of life.

– Amit Gupta

THE CYCLE OF GRACE

We are born into a pretty good deal. Our planet, Earth, is abundant in water and soil, gets plenty of sunlight and oxygen is free for all. It is a beautiful place for life to flourish. Being born on Earth is an all-inclusive trip, where (if the inhabitants are mindful of conserving resources) everything is provided for us to grow and begin to create. There's no suitcase to pack, no hair dryer to bring. We literally show up with nothing, except for one thing...our potential. Just like the acorn has the inherent potential to become an oak tree, we have the essentials within us to grow and blossom into unique human beings, each with our own special talents and characteristics that hold the potential to give back to life in the same way that all of nature does. We are born into what I call the "Cycle of Grace." All of life is constantly giving both of itself and to itself. Life is self-sustaining; whole and complete within itself. We are life. Human beings. In our human-ness, we receive all that we need, so that in our being-ness, we can give all that we are. This may sound strange, but what if we are on this planet to give of ourselves the way an apple tree gives apples, or the way that bees give honey? What if our most natural qualities, talents and brilliance are our gifts to share with other sentient beings?

What is Grace? Grace is a gift of the Divine that is unearned and unmerited. Grace also describes movement that is elegant and flows with ease. To grace someone with your presence means to honor him/her just by being in close proximity to him/her. The "Cycle of Grace" is when Divine gifts flow through you and honor the presence of another.

What if the measure of our success was in the pleasure of creating and sharing rather than the quest to be wealthy, famous, well-liked or highly educated? It is our conceptual self that works for the accolades and riches. Our authentic self knows, in each moment, how to give exactly what is needed with no regard for recognition or reward. If life is self-sustaining, and all beings are created to give, then who should ever be in need?

❧

Find a quiet place to sit where you're not likely to be disturbed.

Take five slow, deep breaths and consider:

What is your gift to life?

Using the Astrology chart in the toolbox (pp. 148-149), find your "Lesson to Master." How can this lesson aid you in sharing your gift?

❧

What is your gift to life?

Using the Astrology chart in the toolbox, find your "Lesson to Master". How can this lesson aid you in sharing your gift?

TOOLBOX
FOR THE
CREATOR'S GIFT

THE STARS AND THE ELEMENTS

Sun Sign: Your sun sign is based on the position of the sun on the day you were born. There are 12 sun signs.

Elements: There are four elements in Astrology: Fire, Earth, Air, and Water.
 Fire signs: Aries, Leo, and Sagittarius
 Air signs: Gemini, Libra, and Aquarius
  Fire and air signs are active or yang and their energy moves outward.
 Earth signs: Taurus, Virgo, and Capricorn
 Water signs: Cancer, Scorpio, and Pisces
  Earth and water signs are receptive or yin and their energy is turned inward.

Imagine using a knob to control your element, applying different levels of the element for different situations. If you are a fire sign think, "would I use the same amount of fire to cook an egg as I would to fry chicken?" What this means is that sometimes you need the creative power of fire when you are beginning a project and you need lots of energy, but when you are spending time with your spouse or children be mindful to turn your fire down as to enjoy a more peaceful home life. Remember: too much fire consumes or incenerates, too much earth buries and conceals, too much air overwhelms and destroys, and too much water drowns and decays. Learn to control your element.

Modalities: There are three modalities in Astrology: Cardinal, Fixed, and Mutable. **Cardinal** signs begin each season and carry an energy of initiation. **Fixed** signs fall in the middle of each season and carry an energy of maintenance and preservation. **Mutable** signs fall at the end of each season and carry the energy of transformation.

Liberating Characteristics: The characteristics of the zodiac sign that assist a soul in mastering their life lessons.

Challenging Characteristics: The characteristics of the zodiac sign that assist a soul in mastering their life lessons via suffering for themselves and others.

Lessons to Master: The lessons we were born to master are directly related to overcoming the challenging aspects of our sun sign and other challenging aspects within our birth chart.

To use this chart, please find your date of birth on this page and follow the row across to find your sun sign, element, and modality. To find the liberating and challenging aspects of your sign and the lesson(s) to master, please continue to follow the row across to the next page.

Date of Birth	Sun Sign	Element	Modality
21st March – 21st April	Aries	Fire	Cardinal
22nd April – 21st May	Taurus	Earth	Fixed
22nd May – 20th June	Gemini	Air	Mutable
21st June – 23rd July	Cancer	Water	Cardinal
24th July – 23rd Augus	Leo	Fire	Fixed
24th August – 23rd September	Virgo	Earth	Mutable
24th September – 23rd October	Libra	Air	Cardinal
24th October – 23rd November	Scorpio	Water	Fixed
24th November – 20th December	Sagittarius	Fire	Mutable
21st December – 20th January	Capricorn	Earth	Cardinal
21st January – 18th February	Aquarius	Air	Fixed
19th February – 20th March	Pisces	Water	Mutable

Liberating Characteristics	Challenging Characteristics	Lessons to Master
Courageous, Energetic, Creative, Initiating	Domineering, Impatient, Arrogant, Impulsive	Unconditional Love
Easy-going, Reliable, The patience of nature, Enduring	Stubborn, Materialistic, Calculating, Insecure	Service to Others
Mentally agile, Funny, Playful, Good Communicator	Gossipy, Superficial, Uncommitted, Spreading oneself too thin	Brotherhood through wisdom and right relation
Caring, Nurturing, Supportive, Awareness of others needs	Manipulative, Emotionally insecure, Jealous, Moody	Peace/ Finding your inner light
Creative, Generous, Self-Confident, Loyal, Inspiring to others	Self-Righteous, Extravagant, Bossy, Self-Centered	Heart-centered Leadership
Conscientious, Cautious, Analytical, Has foresight, Independent	Over critical, ruled by routine, intolerant of others imperfections, Self-inhibited	Understanding Divine Law
Fair, Uniting, Diplomatic, Communicative, Gentle	Emotionally dishonest, Judgmental, Indecisive, Dazzled by appearance	Brotherhood through harmony, balance
Introspective, Seeker of truth, Determined, Self-sufficient	Extreme, Stubborn, Defensive, Self-Destructive, Secretive	Transforming Dark to Light / Peace of Spirit
Visionary, Freedom loving, Inspiring, Jovial, Independent	Melodramatic, Self-Righteous, Explosive temper, Self-Centered	Finding freedom of the Spirit / Uplift Humanity in Truth
Spirit of Mastery, Reliable, Initiating, Hard Working, Determined	Shrewd, Too Serious, Craves Status/Power, Materialistic	Knowledge of the Divine as Source/Use your work for the greater good
Selfless, Hopeful, Creative problem solver, Curious, Believes the best for others	Hypocritical, Opinionated, Stubborn, Ignores the negative in self	Brotherhood through friendliness and compassion
Sensitive, Uses wisdom of the heart, Imaginative, Humble, Gracious	Victim Consciousness, Passive, Undisciplined, Easily Overwhelmed	Understanding & Empathy on a Universal Level

Bibliography / Reference / Citation Page

Bailey, Alice A./Theosophical Society. *Esoteric Astrology*

Pressfield, Steven. *The War of Art.* Black Irish Press, *2012*

The Thief, The Old Lady, and the Friendly Neighbor (Adapted from CrashCourse, "Metaethics: Crash Course Philosophy #32 and "A Reversal Test on Moral Luck, and a Defence of Virtue Ethics", By Marcus Teo")

Wannabe Artist: Spice Girls / Album: Spice / Released: 1996 / Songwriter(s): Spice Girls; Matt Rowe; Richard Stannard

Illustration credits

Cover Image: Bigstock/Shutterstock
Interior graphics: Luke Carter (Fiverr.com)
Map: Pixabay
Pine Trees, clip-art

Colophon

Sakash Publishing, 2019, St. Louis, MO
www.rashannon.com

About the Author

Rachel A. Shannon is an author, spiritual companion, and adventurer. When she isn't writing, you might find Rachel traveling, facilitating Autology workshops, spending time with family and close friends, or admiring nature with her sidekick, Pixie the Pit Bull.

R.A. Shannon also writes for children and has crafted an adventure story titled *Autumn Lee & Her Fantabulous Flying Pants*.

Rachel is on a life-long mission to alleviate suffering by directing people toward their inner-wisdom, authenticity, and unaffected power. For more information on spiritual companioning or workshops visit R.A. Shannon's official website: www.rashannon.com

www.ingramcontent.com/pod-product-compliance
Lightning Source LLC
Chambersburg PA
CBHW081330090426
42737CB00017B/3076